CW00693174

britney spears

confidential

First published in Great Britain in 2001 by

Virgin Books

An imprint of

Virgin Publishing Ltd

Thames Wharf Studios

Rainville Road

London W6 9HA

Copyright © 2000 Virgin Publishing Ltd

Text by Molly MacDermot

The right of Molly MacDermot to be identified as the author of this work
has been asserted by her in accordance with the Copyright,
Designs and Patents Act, 1988.

This book is sold subject to the condition that it shall not, by way of trade or otherwise,
be lent, resold, hired out or otherwise circulated without the publisher's prior written
consent in any form or binding other than that in which it is published and without a
similar condition being imposed upon the subsequent purchaser.

A catalogue record for the book is available from the British Library.

ISBN 0 7535 0551 7

Printed and bound in Spain by Bookprint, S.L. Barcelona

Set in Helvetica

Colour Origination by Colourwise Ltd

Designed by Balley Design Associates

This book is not sponsored or authorized by,
or affiliated in any way with Britney Spears.

the unofficial book

britney spears

confidential

molly macdermot

Virgin

Contents

with two backup dancers in shopping malls across the US. The response was tremendous; people were intrigued by her and wanted to know more about this fresh, new talent who was wowing them with her combination of song and dance. It didn't take long for a buzz to generate, as word of mouth got around that there was a cool new kid on the block. By the time her single '… Baby One More Time' was released on 23 October 1998, there was already a growing fan base – Britney was on the brink of becoming a star.

Tour life has changed dramatically for Britney since that mall gig in 1998. For starters, she's not as nervous about performing, and has become used to seeing the crowds with their posters and homemade signs fluttering throughout the stadium.

She's discovered that she will never again wonder what it is like to be loved by her fans.

Now that she's performing in her own elaborate headlining tours and singing and dancing to her hit songs in huge stadiums around the world, Britney can't help but feel amazed. Her shows have blown up into elaborate productions that Britney had only dreamed about. Now that she's been touring for over two years, she's much more comfortable presenting her music. She's also been touring with the same people for so long that she's grown to love them like family.

In a nutshell, a Britney Spears concert is pure fun. Experiencing Britney live gives you an unmistakable adrenaline rush – and it's hard to fall asleep later without replaying the evening's show in your head. Can you imagine how hard it must be for Britney to wind down? As soon as she says goodbye to the crowd, she sprints on the tour bus parked behind the stadium, and, still out of breath from the performance, she tries to get in a good night's sleep before doing the same thing all over again the following day. Quite simply, tour life for Britney is like running a marathon.

A typical concert begins around 8 p.m., about the time fans flock to their seats in the sold-out stadium – which can often hold up to fifty thousand people. Britney's opening acts get the audience revved up with their own blend of new music. A number of talented groups and solo acts have graced the stage during Britney's sold-out tours, such as the British trio BBMak, Steps, Five, Nobody's Angel, 2gether – the spoof boy band from MTV – and the girl group Innosense. Incidentally, Britney had originally joined Innosense before pursuing a solo career. Another interesting fact is that Justin Timberlake's mother, Lynn Harless, manages Innosense. Countless other artists who have opened for her have all contributed in their own way to making a Britney concert complete. For the lucky supporting groups who are chosen for such a huge tour, it's a major career boost to snag such a highly coveted spot. It gives them that tremendous exposure to reach a mainstream audience. Britney remembers feeling privileged – and lucky – when she landed the opening gig on the 'N Sync tour in late 1998. It was a once-in-a-lifetime opportunity to reach out to thousands of potential fans.

Once the final opening act wraps up their last song at a Britney concert, the fans' cheers begin to build and, before long, everyone is standing up for the wave: that's when rows and rows of audience members jump up with their hands held high to create a falling-domino effect. Growing more and more impatient to see their star emerge from backstage, the audience begin screaming the name that was invented for chanting, 'Brit-*ney!* Brit-*ney!*'

As the sun sets, fans wave their glow sticks in the night air, creating the effect of a fluorescent green sea filling the stadium. Permeating the air are the sweet-smelling candy and buttery popcorn smells wafting from the concession stands. Gaudy beach balls bounce from one fan's outreached hand to the next. Some creative supporters dress up for the show wearing looks inspired by Britney's videos, such as her sassy school uniform in '… Baby One More Time', her sparkling green tube top in 'Crazy' and her head-to-toe white get-up in 'Sometimes'. Dressing like Britney is a way for fans to pay tribute to their stylin' star.

Some concertgoers come to the show with armloads of flowers, notes and care packages in the hope of hand-delivering their gifts backstage to the star of the evening.

There's not one person in the crowd who isn't desperate to meet Britney up close. Some lucky fans have won tickets to attend the meet-and-greets with Britney before the concert.

Others keep their fingers crossed that they'll get their own glimpse of the star coming out of her tour bus. Britney is usually welcomed by a group of excited fans waiting by the gates for her arrival. After slowing down so as not to hurt anyone, the bus peels into the restricted-parking area behind the stage so Britney can hop off and start preparing for the show. It's easy to figure out if Britney is in town because her entourage includes at least ten buses to transport the band, the dancers and the rest of her 'dream team', as she calls it.

As the excitement grows in the stadium, Britney pumps herself up backstage for her grand entrance. Everyone is sitting on the edge of their seat trying to guess which Britney hit will start the evening. Will it be the get-out-of-your-seat-and-dance song 'Crazy'? Or will she treat the audience to '…Baby One More Time' from the get-go? Then the topic turns to Britney's clothes. What will this fashion diva wear next? Will it be a crop-top made of silver sequins? Or will she float on stage engulfed in fluffy white boa feathers, as she has in the past?

Just when the fans can't stand the suspense another second, Britney's five-piece band, made up of Skip, Freddy, Slam, Dan and Mike, take their cue and build the bass to a pounding rhythm, echoing a heartbeat. Britney's band keep a low profile, but she graciously thanked them in the liner notes of *Oops! ... I Did It Again.* She wrote that they're 'five of the best guys whom I couldn't do without'.

Just as the screams reach jet-engine proportions, the fans finally get what they've been waiting for. Britney emerges on stage. For over an hour and a half, fans are transported to Britney's world of set transformations, complicated dance routines and enough smash songs to satisfy the tens of thousands of fans. Britney often gives an encore, thanks the audience and then – whoosh! – the evening is over.

This is just a glimpse of one of Britney's shows, but, as every true concert fan knows, nothing beats witnessing this pop princess with your own two eyes. It's her talent for performing that makes her tours some of the most celebrated and successful musical events in history. Her shows get sold out in minutes and fans have been known to do anything for tickets, including camping out for days in freezing cold weather.

Following the release of her second album, Britney kicked off her 'Oops! ... I Did It Again' summer tour and performed to one of her largest audiences yet, selling out 20,000-plus-seat stadiums from New York to California in a flash.

The tour had lots of surprises, for both the fans and Britney. For starters, Britney, who always travels with an eight-person dance team, replaced three of her dancers on the tour with Ryan, Bryan and Gil, who danced with Janet Jackson. Her previous dancers, Andre, TJ and Alex, who had been working with Britney from the very beginning, left to advance their careers with new creative projects. Although Britney remains close to her original dancers, it was an emotional time when she had to say goodbye to a part of her team who had been with her from the beginning.

Britney has a good eye for picking amazing dancers, and it didn't take long for fans to applaud the new guys for their gravity-defying flips and fancy footwork.

Another surprise came from Britney: she decided it was time for her own tour bus. With all the pressure riding on the new album and its tour, Britney took every step to make sure she was in top form. That would require her to get the essential downtime she needed to recharge her battery for each night's performance. For her previous tours, she has shared a bus with her dancers and had special times with them talking to all hours of the night, playing cards or watching movies. She knew that she needed a change and set out to create a home away from home. After all, she spends most of her time on a tour bus – so she decided it was time to decorate the bus to make it feel more like her own home. Another inside scoop: Britney fills her bus with huge lollipops, which have become a fave tour treat.

Lynne knew her tireless daughter needed an outlet for her energies, so she enrolled her in ballet class at Renée Donewar's School of Dance, an hour away from Kentwood in New Orleans. It was in that small studio that Britney took her first dance steps. In fact, those standard ballet positions have provided the foundation for Britney's now complicated choreography. If you watch her steps carefully, you can see her feet, legs and arms following the ballet training that was drilled into her from an early age.

Britney's dance teacher noticed that her student was a natural after just a few classes and she told Lynne that her daughter was a talented girl who could not only dance but also sing. It's her versatility for song and dance that solidifies Britney's successful performances and has allowed her to rise above the competition. The teacher recommended that Britney explore her talents with recitals and local shows. Britney did just that, performing at any event that came up, including Berry Day, a talent show that allows Kentwood talents an outlet for their creativity.

Two years of dance class only whetted her appetite for more and before long Britney was diving head first into gymnastics class, where she learned many of the moves she now displays in her videos, such as her jaw-dropping tumbles and back flips. Even as a kid, Britney had a strong work ethic, so, once school was over for the year and summer kicked in, she knew she needed a challenge. She begged her parents to let her train in Houston under the famous Olympic gymnastics coach Bela Karolyi, who fashioned the legendary Nadia Comaneci into a winner of Olympic gold.

Today, Britney's passions continue to drive her to perfection – she's tireless about rehearsing her steps and songs, as her crew know – and she was no different growing up. In fact, she would cry buckets of tears if she had to miss gymnastics class; she refused to fail at anything she put her mind to. But after struggling to reach the top Britney realized she was not destined to be the future gymnastics star at the Olympics. Her talents were forged in the specific combination of dance and song; it made sense that she make the switch from the gym floor to the stage. Even at eight, Britney was on the track to becoming the multi-talented performer she wanted to be. Surprisingly, Britney admits she has a shy side, but those early days of talent competitions and weekly performances in the church choir gave

her the confidence to perform publicly. Now, she draws from the wealth of knowledge that she gained from these experiences. This is especially true when she has to get on stage and perform a song during an event as big as the 42nd Annual Grammy Awards.

Although she still gets nervous before a big crowd, she's learned how to dodge potential pitfalls and face the world head on by working hard on her material and believing in herself.

The constant – one thing Britney continues to excel at – is that she performs well under pressure.

Growing up in a small town has also boosted Britney's creativity. She had the peace and quiet to work on her own unique style without many distractions or outside influences. Britney has joked that there are lots of cows in her quiet hometown, and not much else. The nearest McDonald's is fifteen minutes away by car and the mall is at least an hour away. To her benefit, she had the time to imagine her dreams. She remembers many instances when she would gaze out of the window, deep in thought, picturing herself performing for a large audience.

Her small-town upbringing meant close ties with fellow residents, and it wasn't uncommon for folks to stop by the Spears household for a friendly chat and delivery of home-baked goods such as Mississippi Mud Pie. In fact, she could just skip next door to visit her grandparents for heart-to-heart talks and a slice of apple pie. Britney has said that everyone in Kentwood knows each other – and their business – so the town backed her with loving support and encouragement during her local performances. Even now they welcome the pop star home with 'Welcome Home' signs. They even gave Kentwood the nickname 'Spears County'. In fact, Kentwood officials added a slogan to the town's welcome sign that says 'Home of Britney Spears'. Even though Britney has had a taste of the more glamorous cities such as London, New York and Paris, Kentwood has always been her home base, her retreat.

Winning first prize at talent shows and gaining the public exposure she craved was fairly easy on her own home turf. It propelled little Brinnie to continue her interests with enthusiasm, but she certainly wasn't without her obstacles, her disappointments. Britney will never forget the first time she auditioned for *The New Mickey Mouse Club* in 1990, when she was eight. Lynne was reading the newspaper one morning when her eyes fell on an announcement. The Disney variety show, which had originally aired in the 1950s, was making a big comeback and needed new 'Mouseketeers' to make up the cast for the new season. She mentioned the ad to Britney, and, not surprisingly, the eight-year-old was excited. She persuaded her mother to drive her to the audition in Atlanta, Georgia.

After putting on a near flawless performance, Britney was sure she'd get a spot on the show. The producers seemed to love her and she had given the audition everything she had. So it was to her surprise, and great disappointment, when she was deemed too young to join. This wouldn't be the first time in her career when age would play a factor: she would later be criticized as being too young to make a number one album.

Having faced rejection head on, Britney couldn't help but feel deflated and disappointed, so she reluctantly went back home to Kentwood with her mother. Refusing to let a setback get in her way, Britney vowed to keep trying.

She's never been a quitter; she's learned that life is a series of hurdles that need to be overcome.

She follows that philosophy still today. It also wasn't the last time Britney would have to face rejection. In fact, when Britney lost the Best New Artist Award to Christina Aguilera at the 2000 Grammys, she had her coping skills handy. This seasoned professional has had to keep a stiff upper lip on numerous occasions during her career, dispelling the myth that fame has been handed to her on a silver platter.

In front of her family, her friends, her peers, her critics, and, more dramatically, in front of the whole world, Britney handled the Grammy loss gracefully. She has said that she had just given a performance and was backstage when the winner was announced. Her first thought was that she had let down her family, along with all the other people on her team who support her; she knew how much everyone had hoped that she would receive the award. What eased the blow was that she focused on the positive: she had been nominated, and that was more than she had ever imagined. Any performer knows that rejection is part of the business and you can't let one loss stop you from persevering. Britney has said that her mother made her feel better with just the right words. She told her she loved her daughter no matter what.

After her first try at *The New Mickey Mouse Club,* Britney discovered that her audition was not entirely in vain. A producer from the show suggested that the Spears' contact an agent in New York who would be able to help their budding star, so they wasted little time getting on the phone to discuss Britney's future. Accompanied by her mother, who was pregnant with Jamie Lynn at the time, small-town Britney Spears flew to New York City to hone her skills. She took intensive dance classes at the Off-Broadway Dance Center and further explored her talents at Manhattan's Professional Performing Arts School (think of the movie *Fame* and you'll get an idea of the training

much older than the photo on the album cover. Having learned from that, she was adamant about getting an accurate look for the cover of *Oops! … I Did It Again.* She was a perfectionist about finding the right fashion, hair and make-up stylists, who would understand her vision. After all, millions of people now own the CD and look at the photo, so it only makes sense that she would strive for an album cover representative of her current image.

Britney's involvement in her work has been to her benefit because, as history has shown, some new artists fall prey to dishonest people who make the wrong decisions for them. For instance, there have been many VH1 television specials about teen stars from the past who made bad business decisions, were ill-treated by their handlers, and sadly lost all control of their career. Today, artists have learned from their predecessors' mistakes and are therefore much more savvy when it comes to their contracts and other paperwork that trail their every step.

Britney is one of those artists who pay close attention to every detail of their careers.

She makes sure she always surrounds herself with good, trustworthy people who keep her interests a priority.

For the fans who have closely followed Britney's every move since she became the new artist to watch in late 1998, it's obvious how much she has changed. Although she's still the warm-hearted family girl who likes to have fun, she has also come into her own as a strong person, one who takes her work seriously. She has said that she doesn't just want to be known as a teen who likes to sing, dance and swoon for movie stars: she wants her fans to know that below her bubbly exterior is a hard-working girl who is devoted to living her dream, inspiring others to do the same, and putting out music her fans will enjoy.

Remarkably, Britney's gone from a shy, unknown kid from Louisiana to a multi-platinum-selling personality – and she's done her growing up in the watchful public eye. Compare the photo on her debut cover, *… Baby One More Time* with the one on her second album *Oops! … I Did It Again* to see how she's grown up. Sure, she's dyed her hair and experimented with different fashion looks and make-up styles, but what's really different about Britney today is that she's matured musically and personally. She's playing a bigger role in the music she sings and she's showing a healthy supply of confidence. You can see it in her eyes, this girl is happy with herself.

What makes a hit album?

It was easy for us to pick up our first Britney album, slip it into the CD player, and listen to it for hours, but what actually went into making the smash-hit album? Well, Britney had to learn the songs, listen to the demo tape, record it, think of video ideas, promote it, and then wait for the results from the chart shows to see how her music was rating with her fans and the critics. Max Martin had originally written the song '… Baby One More Time' for the R&B trio TLC, but their record label thought it would be better for Five. Martin then decided to take it to Britney so she could sing it, and the rest, as they say, is history.

For her second album, Britney has said that it was easier because she was more experienced, but she did have the added pressure to be a number one artist all over again. To confirm her musical credibility with critics, she included more ballads, such as 'Don't Let Me Be the Last To Know'.

She also wanted her music to reflect her current mood, so she aimed at making it edgier and funkier.

For songs like 'Oops! … I Did It Again' and 'Lucky', she teamed up with Max Martin in Sweden again. *Oops!* sold 1,319 million copies in the first week, so she's clearly found the sound people want to hear!

Britney also recorded in Geneva, Switzerland, with Shania Twain's husband Mutt Lange for 'Don't Let Me Be the Last To Know' and in New York with Rodney Jerkins. She had chatted with Jerkins about collaborating on the album when she was backstage at the 1999 Grammy Award nominations. He told her he wanted to give her a sassier sound, like Janet Jackson's. That, of course, was music to Britney's ears because Janet has been her idol since she started listening to her funky tunes as a kid. Ultimately, Rodney would redo Britney's version of '(I Can't Get No) Satisfaction'.

Ten things you didn't know about Britney

1. Her album *Oops! … I Did It Again* was originally going to be titled *Sunflower*.
2. As everyone knows, she clicked with England's Prince William over email. But what some don't know is that she has English blood in her. Her mother's family still live in parts of England.
3. Like other high-profile stars, Britney has tried to disguise herself with different props so she isn't recognized in public. One time she wore a long black wig (think Cher's hair) at the urging of her dancers. Unfortunately, her disguise didn't work. People noticed her even more than if she had just put on a baseball cap. She has said that it's getting progressively more difficult to go out in public without getting mobbed
4. When she came to New York to start working on her debut album *… Baby One More Time*, her record company, Jive, put her up in an apartment with Fee Culotta. This was her home away from home while she started recording her first album.
5. On 2 December 1998, she celebrated her seventeenth birthday on the tour bus during her opening stint for 'N Sync's tour. Justin, Lance, Joey and Chris sang her a harmonized version of 'Happy Birthday'. She celebrated her eighteenth birthday by singing 'Silent Night' at the Christmas lighting at New York's

Rockefeller Center. Then she headed to the trendy, red-velvet-roped Greenwich Village club, Halo, surrounded by family and friends, including 'N Sync. Every year the public celebrate another year for Britney, wondering what she'll surprise us with next. She was presented with a diamond necklace from Jive Records to commemorate 10 million copies sold of … *Baby One More Time.*

6 One of Britney's most treasured recordings is the song '(I Can't Get No) Satisfaction', which was originally a 1965 hit for the Rolling Stones. Mick Jagger, the lead singer of the group, rarely allows other artists to cover his tunes, but he granted Britney's wish. The reason the song is special for her is that, when her friend first got a car, the two would drive around happily singing 'Satisfaction'. At first people told her not to cover the classic rock number, but she recorded it anyway. She purposely made it different with the help of the producer Rodney Jerkins, so the songs wouldn't be compared to each other. She says she would also like to cover Prince's 1984 hit 'Purple Rain'.

7 Britney's bodyguard, Big Rob (Robert Feggans), takes his job seriously so Britney feels secure. The 350-pound guy benches 380, so he's in top form to watch over Britney's safety. One time, Britney was on a hotel balcony talking privately with her mother when a strange guy leaned over his own balcony and began to take rather too much interest in their conversation. In no time, Big Rob was to the rescue.

8 The residents of Kentwood have created a museum for their famous hometown girl at the request of fans. It's slated to open in 2001. That's right, Britney will have her own museum, which will be a part of the already existing Kentwood Museum. There will be a gift shop and Britney memorabilia. Lynne and Jamie Spears have donated items, such as the necklace she wore at the Mardi Gras parade and the two dresses she wore for her performances on *Star Search.*

9 After picking family and friends first, Britney says the next person she would like to spend the day with is the US talk-show queen Oprah Winfrey because Britney finds her incredibly interesting.

10 When Britney found out she broke records with her first week's sales of *Oops! … I Did It Again*, she was in a studio in Orlando, Florida, rehearsing for her summer tour. Always the hard worker, Britney took a minute's break to hug her manager Johnny Wright and toasted the triumphant feat with a glass of Coca-Cola. Then she got right back to rehearsing.

chapter four

Dear Diary: Her Private Life

Most of the world knows Britney's public persona, the singing, dancing star who smiles brightly for the camera. She radiates a larger-than-life image, one who always seems energetic and on. Britney down? Never, or at least that is how it seems. Remarkably, Britney puts on a brave face even when up against challenges; she is a trooper who puts her fans before herself. Britney is human, however, and well hidden from the public eye is her deeply private side, which she reveals only to those close to her, such as family and friends.

What is this pop princess really like when she's not decked from head to toe in dressy duds, eye-grabbing make-up and perfect hair? As she writes in her confessional song 'Dear Diary', she's an emotional person with deep feelings just like any girl on the planet. She's just like you and me – a human being who likes to enjoy the good things in life.

Britney loves to eat cookie-dough ice cream from the carton, hang out in her night things all day and take long, relaxing bubblebaths.

In fact, when she's at award shows and people ask her to hang out and go to one party after the next, she bows out gracefully because, she has said, she's not a party animal. She'd much rather have a hot bath and a good night's sleep. Britney's also a girl with a great imagination, so, when she has the downtime to think about things other than scheduled interviews, touring and recording, she takes full advantage and dreams about things that make her happy.

One subject that Britney could spend lots of time dreaming about is love. Like many girls, she hopes that one day she'll meet Mr Right, her perfect soul mate, who will sweep her off her feet and take her to a land where she can live happily ever after. In fact, she went to a fortune teller just for fun and was told that she will marry a guy with dark hair when she's 23. She has dreams of living in a beautiful house with a husband and three kids somewhere close to her family in Kentwood. Early marriages run in her family: her brother Bryan, four years older than she, has (at the time of writing) a fiancée, Blaize, and her parents married in

their early twenties. On the topic of marriage, Britney has said that her tastes in guys change as frequently as her tastes in clothes, so she doesn't understand why people marry so young.

Now that Britney is in the limelight, everyone wants to know about her love life, especially sensationalist tabloids. What often happens is that stories get blown out of proportion and Britney is falsely linked with a list of eligible guys. The truth is, Britney has her crushes and, if time permits, she does try to go on the occasional date, but being a pop star isn't always as glamorous as the gossip columns portray it. Britney has said that when she reads the gossip, that she's going out with this guy and that guy, she laughs and thinks, I wish.

One persistent story that won't go away is the one about Britney and Justin Timberlake being in a serious relationship. Gallons of ink have been shed on the subject and it has meant that Britney's personal life has unfairly met intense public scrutiny. Britney has admitted that she and Justin are good friends and enjoy each other's company – and sometimes kiss – but that it is nothing serious. It's understandable why the stories surface: Britney and Justin have been friends since they were eleven on *The New Mickey Mouse Club*. Plus, they've toured together and their paths often cross just because they're in the same business. In reality, however, both Britney and Justin have been working at high speeds to promote their new albums and embark on non-stop tours. What that means is lots of flying around the world, sometimes on a weekly basis with hardly enough time to sleep, let alone maintain a serious relationship. So, it only makes sense to take Britney at her word. She has said she adores Justin, and vice versa, but sometimes a friendship really is just a friendship. Time will tell.

Another bit of juicy hearsay off the grapevine is that Britney is dating the blond Prince William, the first born son of the late Princess Diana, and the heir to the English throne. Although such majestic talk is flattering – Britney confesses she'd love to be dating the Prince – she insists this tall tale is yet another false bit of fodder created by the gossip hounds. The real story is that Britney's record company sent the Prince an autographed photo of Britney when they learned that he's a big fan of her music. He sent a handwritten letter of thanks, which started a brief correspondence of emails between the Prince and Britney. Again, in reality, having Prince William as a casual cyber-

and, when her mother heard it while sitting in the audience, she cried.

When she landed a spot on *The New Mickey Mouse Club*, Britney had to move to Orlando, Florida, where the show was taped, so her mother kept her company with her younger sister Jamie Lynn. And, while there are 'stage mothers' who push their kids to be stars, Britney has always said that her mother would have been happy to have just cooked for and watched over her daughter, but, because Britney showed a passion for performing from the start, Lynne encouraged her.

Britney wanted to find a special way to show her mother how thankful she is for her support and love, so she surprised her with a generous gift that will last a lifetime. She got her mother a new house. It's always been Lynne's dream to move out of the three-bedroom ranch that the family have squeezed into all these years, and move into a more spacious home. Britney is helping her mother's dream come true by hiring contractors to build the Spears family a bigger house on a bigger plot in another section of Kentwood. The house is everything Lynne hoped for: it's built in the Tudor style, with three fireplaces that you can light with a remote control, a luxury device made famous in the movie *Clueless*.

Britney's close relationship with her mother has helped the famous performer stay grounded.

She knows that, if she lets anything get to her head, her mother will keep her in line. That goes for everyone in Britney's family. She remembers pestering her brother by singing and dancing to Madonna songs when they were growing up. When Bryan told Britney to be quiet because he was trying to watch television, she would just roll her eyes at him. That bantering is typical of sibling relationships and Britney wouldn't have it any other way.

Bryan always makes an effort to stop by the house for dinner so he can catch up with his younger sister. Britney also makes a special effort to attend her younger sister's softball games because she knows how important it is to have your family around you during a winning point. Britney used to play too – she was a pitcher – and so she gives Jamie Lynn first-hand advice. When Britney was planning to shoot the video for 'Lucky', she rearranged the plans in order to get the video completed in two days instead of three so she could attend her sister's dance recital. Some music insiders have remarked on the close resemblance between Britney and her kid sis, and some wonder if Jamie Lynn would ever pursue a career in music. For now, Jamie Lynn is happy to focus on sports, according to Britney.

Britney adores her younger sister and has called her a spitfire who has an abundance of confidence. She has said that Jamie Lynn likes to sing along to her songs and even challenges her older sister with singing competitions in the house. For an especially memorable bonding event, Britney joined her family at the Mardi Gras parade, where she served as grand marshal. She spent four hours amid 28 floats, 42 marching bands and thousands of parade-goers.

Video Magic

It's impossible to think of Britney Spears without picturing her visually fantastic videos. She has catapulted herself – high kicks and all – into our homes with jaw-dropping, tear-shedding, smile-inducing abandon. When it comes to videos, Britney's got it. When she pops up on MTV or on *The Box*, the instant reaction is to reach for the remote and up the volume. And that's even after several hundred viewings. In fact, even though MTV has to 'retire' videos after they appear 65 times, fans still request Britney's recordings months after they're released.

Fans say they can't get enough of Britney's slick, sparkling, engrossing videos because they're entertaining, like watching a movie.

That's the same feeling Britney experienced when she first saw Michael Jackson's video for 'Thriller', and she hopes to use that inspiration to create videos others will love for years to come. She has said that she insists on producing well-thought-out videos because, once they appear on MTV and the whole world sees them, they're in people's memories for good. If they're not perfect, that's something Britney can't live with.

When it's announced that Britney is stopping by MTV's *Total Request Live* headquarters, situated right in the middle of New York's bustling Times Square where yellow cabs and crowds of people pack the area, fans line up in front of the big window facing Broadway holding homemade signs pledging their fan loyalty. They're hoping to catch a glimpse of Britney announcing the video countdown with *TRL*'s host Carson Daly in the glass-encased studio. Sometimes, a fan from the crowd is picked to go up to the studio to meet Britney personally.

What makes a Britney video so compelling changes from one clip to the next. With Britney's video debut '... Baby One More Time', which first appeared on *TRL* in November 1999, fans say the schoolroom setting and spirited attitude caught their eye. But what really inspired them to request the video over and over was Britney's dancing.

'... Baby One More Time' was supposed to be an entirely different video than we see now. The first treatment presented to Britney was an animated video featuring Power Ranger-type characters. Britney

thought the concept was too juvenile: she wanted her debut video to be edgy and daring. One day, while sitting on a plane, Britney had a brainwave that would solve all the problems with her video. She visualized a school setting with lots of dancing, so she told her record company about it and they phoned the British director Nigel Dick, who is known for his cutting-edge creations. He was already experienced with pop music, having directed Backstreet Boys' video for 'As Long As You Love Me'. Britney also had a say in the casting. She asked her cousin Chad, who was working as a model for Abercrombie & Fitch, to play the love interest, and she asked her chaperone Fee to play the teacher. For two days the crew worked feverishly getting the shots perfect at Rydell High School in Venice, California, where the movie Grease was filmed. As is typical of video shoots, there was lots of downtime, so the girls on the set played cards and board games while the guys kicked around a soccer ball. All the hard work paid off because the video turned out to be one of the most requested on MTV.

Britney's second video, for 'Sometimes', didn't run as smoothly. Britney's notorious knee accident came at the worst time, just as she was in the middle of rehearsing her dance steps for 'Sometimes'. It was February of 1999, a month after her album went number one and her life started getting crazy, when Britney was in a Los Angeles studio doing a step that required her to lift her leg high in the air. As she did, her standing leg buckled and she badly twisted her knee. When she first went to the doctor to check on the seriousness of her accident, she was told it would be fine with the help of a physiotherapist. But, when the pain persisted after a few days, she went to a specialist doctor at the New Orleans Doctors' Hospital who had to remove the torn cartilage. When the doctor told her she needed surgery she remembers bursting into tears.

Unfortunate mishaps never come at a good time, but this accident hit Britney just as she was in the middle of a high-powered month of activities. She was scheduled to finish her video, attend the Forty-first Annual Grammy Awards, and kick off a promotional tour throughout Britain, but her plans were changed so she could recover for the designated six weeks. Britney has said that it was a terrible time because she's such an energetic person and hated having to be in a wheelchair and on crutches when she really wanted to be dancing.

Fortunately, the video turned out to be a success, although the

ballad didn't climb the charts as high as her debut. 'Sometimes' was shot in Malibu, California, at the beach, but ironically the weather was freezing. Britney mustered up her acting skills to make it look convincingly warm and pleasant. The video, directed again by the trendy British director Nigel Dick, features Britney by the boardwalk contemplating a lost love. Considering she had recently hurt her knee, the dance scenes on the boardwalk are fairly demanding. While '... Baby One More Time' was a racier video, 'Sometimes' tried to present a softer, more innocent side of Britney. She wears all white in most of the scenes and her hair and make-up are subtle.

Britney's video for '(You Drive Me) Crazy' was her biggest yet, production-wise. It was also her most exhausting to shoot because she had so much going on: a live show the day of the video, and MTV was on the set shooting a documentary about the making of the video. True to Britney's personality, she remained calm and got the job done. The shoot took place in a converted warehouse in Los Angeles, made to look like a retro diner with green and red neon signs, rollerblading waitresses and lots of extras dancing in the background. The video also included cameo appearances by Melissa Joan Hart and Adrian Grenier, who starred in the romance comedy *Drive Me Crazy*.

Fans liked the up-tempo song and the high-energy dancing, and the video became yet another MTV fave.

Following the flashing lights and explosions of 'Crazy' was the sweet ballad 'From the Bottom of My Broken Heart'. The video, awash in sunflowers, swings and plenty of greenery was given the same soft glow by its director, Gregory Dark, as he gave to Mandy Moore's ballet-inspired video 'I Wanna Be With You'.

Filmed in a Los Angeles suburb, Britney's fourth US video features a hat-clad Britney displaying remarkable thespian powers as she tells the story of a girl who has to leave her family and boyfriend to go to college. Britney alternates the pace of her videos, going from up-tempo to ballad in a smooth succession. To make the point, 'From the Bottom Of My Broken Heart' was followed by the loud, fast, 'Oops! ... I Did It Again', which certainly proved to be her most challenging video effort yet.

For this first single from her new album, she was determined to present a far-out video to accompany the edgy, electric sounds of 'Oops! ... I Did It Again'. So she called the director Nigel Dick once more, to work his magic the way he had for '... Baby One More Time'. The now highly sought-after director has said that Britney just called him up one day and told him exactly what she had in mind for the video. She envisioned a space-age feel for her new video, which was to be set on another planet, specifically the fiery, tempestuous Mars. She also requested that the video feature a cute guy who would star as her counterpart, and she suggested there be no spaceships. The director also had to work in the *Titanic* dialogue, which on the album is actually Britney and Max Martin speaking. The British director homed in on the space-age themes to create one of the most multi-layered video productions ever.

Britney worked with the choreographer Tina Landin, who has supplied her with fabulous dance sequences in the past. Always her own stuntwoman, Britney herself supplied the awe-inspiring back flips and spinning.

In mid-March of 2000, Britney and crew met at Universal Studios in Studio City, California, where they would work from 16 to 18 March to make the video. Most videos take a maximum of two days to complete, so fans knew they could expect an elaborate video due to the extra day. The crew had no idea how much work would be involved and what strange events would unfold. At least the crew didn't know, but Britney had a hunch. She has said that she has good instincts and had a gut feeling something wasn't right when she woke up to work on the video that day. In fact, she felt drowsy as she was getting ready but didn't want to slow down the production. They had to finish the video that day and they were already behind schedule. But now we're getting ahead of our story.

Costumes are always important in a video, so Britney wanted to wear an eye-catching vinyl catsuit in candy-apple red to play on the fiery aspect of Mars. She also wanted retro hair and make-up, like Heather Graham in *Austin Powers: The Spy Who Shagged Me.* Her long, blonde, highlighted locks required time-intensive hair extensions, and the make-up look was achieved with 1960s-inspired psychedelic blue eye shadow (Britney loves blue). Just when everything seemed to be set, and she was in full costume trying out her dance steps for the camera, Britney noticed something wasn't right.

Her outfit turned out to be more problematic than she predicted. The tight catsuit flattened her front so much that stylists had to insert fake, padded breasts into the suit. With every turn that Britney made, the padding would slip lower and lower until the breasts would fall down, so she frequently had to take a break from shooting so the stylists could sew the padding in place. Then, she realized that vinyl is in fact very hot to wear, so after hours and hours of redoing her dance steps over and over for the camera, Britney noticed that as she did a spin or any type of movement with her arm, sweat would spray out of the bottom of her sleeves. This wasn't exactly the special effect she was looking for, so adjustments had to be made.

The scariest part of the shoot occurred during a complicated scene. For one shot, Britney had to lie down under an overhead camera that would zoom in and out. As she looked up, a big metal piece from the camera fell five feet and hit her on the head. She was knocked out, but when she came to she still insisted on continuing with the shot. It wasn't until a member of the crew saw blood that Britney realized she was actually bleeding from the head and needed to be checked out. A doctor was called to the set and Britney ended up needing four stitches. Because of the effects of concussion she began to feel sick, so the workaholic finally took a rest for about four hours.

Nigel Dick has said that he hopes an accident like that never happens again on his set. He shut down production for a few hours while Britney got help – and some rest – so she could continue. Britney is a trooper who would rather spend the time and energy getting the job done than to feel sorry for herself.

A lot was riding on Britney's shoulders during the shoot. She knew she had to catch a flight the next morning at 4.30 to make another performance, so they had to finish the video that day. Plus, during all the chaos after the accident, the set was full of random reporters and cameramen covering the behind-the-scenes shooting of the video. Even MTV's team was there, filming every detail, including the accident. Fortunately, the MTV producers decided against showing Britney's injury on their show. With all this activity, the now exhausted and injured Britney burst into tears. She has said that a good cry can be cathartic and actually makes her feel totally better. After a cry she asked for a massage, which cleared her mind and

rejuvenated her. She also had a mochaccino, which is one of her fave energy-boosting drinks, to keep her going.

Having fought the frazzled state she was in, Britney got back to work, stitches and all, and finished the video around 1 a.m. – three and a half hours before she had to catch her plane. She has said that she got back to the hotel at 2 a.m., took all her hair extensions and make-up off and had about one hour of sleep before hopping on the plane to get to her performance. Because Britney's afraid of flying, she didn't get much sleep on the plane either. She said that her performance for the show the next day ended up being a winner because, for a change, she directed the remainder of her dwindling energies towards her singing instead of her dancing.

Against all the odds, Britney once again delivered a dynamite video that scaled the top of the video countdown.

For international fans, Britney then released 'Born to Make You Happy', which was directed by Billy Woodruff, who also made Backstreet Boys' 'I'll Never Break Your Heart'.

Luckily, Britney's second video from the *Oops! ... I Did It Again* album went smoothly. On 12 June she drove to Ren-Mar studios in Hollywood, parked her black convertible and got to work on her first day of shooting the video for the poignant song 'Lucky'. The director, David Meyers, envisioned the video to be set in the glamorous 1940s, so Britney wore an old Hollywood-inspired organza nightgown with a long robe, lined with boa feathers. Her hair was styled to look like Veronica Lake, an actress from the 1940s famous for her wavy locks that covered half of her face. At one point in the video, Britney gets up on a billboard wearing a red top and white pants. Her character, Lucky, has a scene with a handsome English guy, played by the actor Nathan James; Britney has said that she likes guys with accents. After lots of hard work, with several different set backgrounds and costume changes, the first day of shooting ended at 2.26 a.m. It was back to work the next day for more costume changes and new make-up looks. Britney has gorgeous pink, sparkling eye shadow on her lids in a few scenes, but, during one particularly dramatic scene, her face is smeared with black mascara to make it look like she's crying. Her character, Lucky, is supposed to be sad and lonely because of the isolating effects of stardom. This fictional character portrays feelings not unlike those that affect Britney from time to time. When asked if she relates to the song, Britney has said in a lot of ways she does. However, she doesn't like it when celebrities complain about their lives.

Britney has said she wouldn't trade her life for anything. She's happy, but does admit there are times when she has bad days, just like everybody else, and sometimes you can be very lonely even when you are surrounded by tons of people.

By 1.28 a.m. the video was complete and Britney, being the loyal older sister that she is, was free to catch the next plane home to Kentwood to see her sister dance.

chapter ten

Fast-Forward To The Future

If you think the past couple of years have been eventful for Britney, wait until you see what this busy girl has planned for the future. For starters, she is already planning her third album, and hopes to devote at least six months to it. That would be the longest amount of time Britney's worked on an album. She also plans on writing more songs after the success of 'Dear Diary' and says she has started learning the guitar to improve her songwriting skills. Britney has been thinking up melodies non-stop – usually while relaxing in the bathtub – and surprisingly, she says, they resemble those of Macy Gray and Sheryl Crow rather than traditional pop.

If it's a case of 'three times lucky', then this next studio effort could even top … *Baby One More Time* and *Oops! … I Did It Again.* Britney has said she would also like to put together a movie like Madonna's *Truth Or Dare*, incorporating her dancers to capture her life on tour.

Along with pursuing her own creative projects, Britney has been asked to collaborate with other artists, namely her good friends from 'N Sync. The idea is for Britney to sing a duet with the guys for their next album, and, according to the group's Lance Bass, the song could quite possibly be the hottest ever.

Along the lines of Janet Jackson and Michael Jackson's duet 'Scream', the Britney/'N Sync collaboration would be edgy and dance oriented.

Britney may also join 'N Sync on the big screen for a movie similar to Britney's self-confessed fave flick, *The Bodyguard*, starring Whitney Houston and Kevin Costner. The romance/comedy could start production as early as the beginning of 2001. Movie scripts have been landing at Britney's feet since she first hit the scene; she has said that she would absolutely love to pursue acting when her music career allows the time for it. Some movie possibilities have included Britney starring in several sequels, such as *Grease 3* and *Dirty*

Dancing 2, as well as the actor Jerry O'Connell's self-penned upcoming movie, *First Daughter.* Britney would play a rebellious daughter of the President of the United States.

Britney may also land the main role as Alice in MTV Films' updated movie version of Lewis Carroll's classic tale *Alice's Adventures in Wonderland.* The modernized script has Alice walking through a city only to be hit by a Volkswagen Rabbit and thrown into an imaginative world where hip-hop and rock 'n' roll music is played. The producers envision Ricky Martin to play the role of the Mad Hatter. Although Britney has been too busy touring to devote herself to a movie, and has had to turn roles down, such as a possible spot in *Scary Movie,* she is now ready to expand her career to include all genres – music, television and movies.

Professionally, Britney will still be busy, but she's said she plans to spend more time on her personal life. That means more trips back home to see her family and watch her younger sister, Jamie Lynn, grow up. This family girl puts her priorities first and has proven that you can be a private person in a public world and still stay grounded. Aside from confirming her place in the musical history books, Britney has reminded each and every one of us that you can reach for the stars, and touch them. That you can have dreams and live them. That it's easy to forget the strength of your passions – you have to believe in yourself.

Quiz: Test your Britney Trivia

1 **Which video was Britney rehearsing for when she twisted her knee?**

    a. '... Baby One More Time'

    b. 'Sometimes'

    c. 'Lucky'

2 **Where did Britney get her fairy tattoo?**

    a. London

    b. Kentwood

    c. New York

3 **Which song did Britney sing for her audition with Jive?**

    a. Whitney Houston's 'I Have Nothing'

    b. Mariah Carey's 'Vision of Love'

    c. Madonna's 'Material Girl'

4 **Which celebrity was not on *The New Mickey Mouse Club* with Britney?**

    a. Keri Russell

    b. Tony Lucca

    c. Joshua Jackson

5 **How old was Britney when she was photographed for her first album *... Baby One More Time?***

    a. 12

    b. 15

    c. 17

6 **What is Britney scared of?**

    a. animals

    b. performing

    c. flying in a plane

7 **Who makes a guest appearance in Britney's video 'Drive Me Crazy'?**

    a. Melissa Joan Hart

    b. Adrian Grenier

    c. Christina Aguilera

8 **Which group did Britney open for in late 1998?**

    a. Backstreet Boys

    b. Spice Girls

    c. 'N Sync

9 **Which group originally recorded '(I Can't Get No) Satisfaction', before Britney?**

    a. Aerosmith

    b. Rolling Stones

    c. Eagles

10 **Which song did Britney and her mother sing in the car that Britney later performed in concert?**

    a. Journey's 'Open Arms'

    b. Madonna's 'Like a Prayer'

    c. Bette Midler's 'Wind Beneath My Wings'

11 Who did Britney call when she won at the American Music Awards?

    a. her manager

    b. her mother

    c. Carson Daly

12 How many awards did Britney win at the MTV European music awards?

    a. 2

    b. 3

    c. 4

13 Who directed her video 'Oops! … I Did It Again'?

    a. Gregory Dark

    b. Stephen Spielberg

    c. Nigel Dick

14 What video did Britney shorten to two days' filming instead of three so she could see her sister's dance recital?

    a. 'Lucky'

    b. 'From the Bottom of My Broken Heart'

    c. '… Baby One More Time'

15 What do most fans wave in the air at Britney's concerts?

    a. flags

    b. posters

    c. glow sticks

16 Who did Britney meet for dinner at Planet Hollywood in Los Angeles?

    a. Brad Pitt

    b. Enrique Iglesias

    c. Ben Affleck

17 Britney's astrological sign is:

    a. Sagittarius

    b. Aquarius

    c. Leo

18 What candy does Britney especially like and keep on her tour bus?

    a. giant lollipops

    b. chocolate bars

    c. mints

19 Where did Britney spend her eighteenth-birthday party?

    a. a New York club

    b. her tour bus

    c. in Kentwood

20 What has helped Britney realize her dreams?

    a. the support of her family

    b. her fans loyalty

    c. her own dedication and drive

Answers: 1. b; **2.** c; **3.** a; **4.** c; **5.** b; **6.** c; **7.** a & b; **8.** c; **9.** b; **10.** a; **11.** b; **12.** c; **13.** c; **14.** a; **15.** c; **16.** c; **17.** a; **18.** a; **19.** a; **20.** all of them

Discography

Singles

'... Baby One More Time'
Jive, released November 1998

'... Baby One More Time'
BMG International, released February 1999
Highest Chart Position: 1

'Sometimes'
Jive, released April 1999
Highest Chart Position: 14

'Crazy'
Jive, released September 1999
Highest Chart Position: 10

'From the Bottom of My Broken Heart'
Jive, released February 2000
Highest Chart Position: 14

'Oops! ... I Did It Again'
Jive, released May 2000
Highest Chart Position: 9

'Lucky'
Jive, released August 2000

Albums

Oops! ... I Did It Again
Jive, released 16 May 2000
Highest Chart Position: 1
Tracks: 'Oops! ... I Did It Again', 'Stronger', Don't Go Knockin' On My Door', '(I Can't Get No) Satisfaction', 'Don't Let Me Be the Last To Know', 'What U See (Is What U Get)', 'Lucky', 'One Kiss From You', 'Where Are You Now', 'Can't Make You Love Me', 'When Your Eyes Say It', 'Dear Diary'

... Baby One More Time
Jive, released January 1999
Highest Chart Position: 1

... Baby One More Time
BMG International, released February 1999
Highest chart position: 1
Tracks: '... Baby One More Time', '(You Drive Me) Crazy', 'Sometimes', 'Soda Pop', 'Born To Make You Happy', 'From the Bottom of My Broken Heart', 'I Will Be There', 'I Will Still Love You', 'Thinkin' About You', 'E-mail My Heart', 'The Beat Goes On'

Write to Britney:

The Britney Beat
PO Box 192730
San Francisco, CA 94119-2730

Or visit her website at:

www.britney.com and www.britneyspears.com

Picture Credits
All Action
46; Dave Hogan 13, 71, 75; J.K. 91; Paul Smith 96
AllStar/Globe Photos
78, 83
Alpha
19, 21, 25, 31, 36, 45, 56, 58, 66, 67, 73, 92; Mark Allan 81
Alpha/Globe
15; Steve Finn 9, 54, 70
Corbis
Beckers 41; Steve Rach Mirarchi 88; Reuters New Media Inc 26, 35, 39, 72, 87
Famous
Fred Duval 74

Globe Photos
Fitzroy Barrett 14, 37, 53; Henry McGee 32, 50, 57, 59, 69, 80; Nina Prommer 16, 43
Retna
Larry Busacca 11, 17, 47, 79; M.B. Charles 23; Bill Davila 29; Kevin Estrada 18, 60; Steve Granitz 34, 77 Steve Jennings 39; Sandra Johnson 33, 62, 86, 95 Eddie Malluk 55; Walter McBride 6
South Beach Photo Agency
4, 10, 24, 30, 61, 76
Starfile
Mark Harlan 20, 42, 49, 82, 89; Todd Kaplan 7, 8 Jeffrey Mayer 63; VDL 68, 90